how2become.com

Army Aptitude Tests:
Error Analysis & Number Reasoning

Practice Tests for the British Army Assessment Centre

www.How2Become.com

As part of this product you have also received FREE access to online tests that will help you to pass the Army Aptitude Tests:

To gain access, simply go to:

www.MyPsychometricTests.co.uk

Get more products for passing any test at:

www.How2Become.com

Orders: Please contact How2Become Ltd, Suite 1, 60 Churchill Square Business Centre, Kings Hill, Kent ME19 4YU.

You can order through Amazon.co.uk under ISBN: 9781912370665, via the website www.How2Become.com or through Gardners.com.

ISBN: 9781912370665

First published in 2019 by How2Become Ltd.

Typeset by Gemma Butler for How2Become Ltd.

CONTENTS

Introduction

Welcome to *Army Aptitude Tests: Error Analysis & Number Reasoning*. This guide contains lots of sample test questions that are appropriate for anyone who is applying to join the British Army.

The selection test for the army is designed to assess potential Armed Forces personnel's 'suitability' for specific posts. The higher scores you achieve, the more job opportunities you will have at your disposal. Whilst the minimum pass mark for entry into the army is 26, a candidate will need to score far higher if he or she wishes to join a regiment such as the Royal Electrical and Mechanical Engineers.

The key to success is to try your hardest to get 100% correct answers in the test that you are undertaking. If you aim for 100% in your preparation, then you are far more likely to achieve the trade or career that you want.

We have supplied you with lots of sample questions to assist you. It is crucial that when you get a question wrong, you take the time to find out why you got it wrong.

Understanding the question is very important. You will find that the more practice you undertake in the build up to the real test, the better you will perform on the day.

Please note that the tests in this book are not an exact replication of those that you will sit as part of the Army Aptitude Tests. These tests are designed to assess the same skills that you will need in order to pass the real Army Aptitude Tests. So, while these tests may differ from those that you will face in the exam, improving your abilities in these tests will still prepare you for the Army Aptitude Tests.

In addition to the tests within this guide we would also like to give you free access to our online psychometric testing facility.

To gain access to our suite, simply go to the following website:

www.PsychometricTestsOnline.co.uk

Good luck and best wishes,

The how2become team

The How2Become Team

Error Analysis

Error analysis tests assess your attention to detail, and your ability to spot patterns of information in a short period of time. The format of the test is relatively simple: you'll be given a series of questions, each containing lines of shapes and figures. Each will have 4 rows, with a pattern on each side of the row - one on the right-hand side and one on the left-hand side. Essentially, your task is to establish whether the right-hand side matches up with the left-hand side. There are four of these for each question.

Below we've provided you with an example of how this might look:

So, you can see that there are four rows of code. On row 1, you need to check and see if the left-hand side matches up exactly with the right-hand side. You then need to do the same for rows 2, 3, and 4. In the above question, you can see that the left-hand side of row 1, and the right-hand side of row 1, are exactly the same. The same applies to row 2. However, rows 3 and 4 both have at least one symbol different on the left-hand side, compared to the right-hand side.

You will have 30 seconds to memorise each question, and establish which rows have matching codes on the right and the left. Once you've finished looking at the lines of code, you will need to turn the page, and answer questions based on what you've seen. You will not be able to turn back to the codes. There will be two questions for each set of codes. So, for the above example question, you'll be given something similar to this:

Example Question

a) How many rows had all IDENTICAL symbols?

b) Which row(s) had NON-IDENTICAL symbols?

To answer this, you need to use your memory of the lines of the codes. So, we can remember that the first 2 rows had all matching codes. This means that the answer to the first question would be 2 - there are 2 rows total with matching codes.

When answering the second question, you need to be more careful. Notice that this question asks you WHICH rows had non-identical symbols. Therefore, you need to name the exact rows which didn't match up on the right and left. The answer, in this case, is 3 and 4. Neither row 3, nor row 4, had matching codes.

The above should give you a good idea of how to handle these types of tests. Not only do you need to memorise which rows matched on both sides, and which didn't, but you also need to be careful with the wording of the questions. Remember too that the questions will switch around, so sometimes you may be asked to identify which rows were identical on both sides, and other times you may be asked to identify how many rows were identical, and vice versa with non-identical.

TEST 1 WILL BEGIN ON THE NEXT PAGE

Error Analysis – Test 1

Look at all 4 rows below. Make a mental note of which rows contain identical symbols and which contain non-identical symbols. Answer one question (part a and part b) at a time. You have 30 seconds before you need to turn over to the next page and answer the questions.

Question 1.

Question 2.

Question 3.

Question 4.

Question 5.

Question 1.

a) How many rows had NON-IDENTICAL symbols?

b) Which row(s) had all IDENTICAL symbols?

Question 2.

a) How many rows had all IDENTICAL symbols?

b) Which row(s) had NON-IDENTICAL symbols?

Question 3.

a) How many rows had NON-IDENTICAL symbols?

b) Which row(s) had all IDENTICAL symbols?

Question 4.

a) How many rows had NON-IDENTICAL symbols?

b) Which row(s) had all IDENTICAL symbols?

Question 5.

a) How many rows had all IDENTICAL symbols?

b) Which row(s) had NON-IDENTICAL symbols?

Question 6.

Question 7.

Question 8.

Question 9.

Question 10.

Question 6.

a) How many rows had all IDENTICAL symbols?

b) Which row(s) had NON-IDENTICAL symbols?

Question 7.

a) How many rows had all IDENTICAL symbols?

b) Which row(s) had NON-IDENTICAL symbols?

Question 8.

a) How many rows had NON-IDENTICAL symbols?

b) Which row(s) had all IDENTICAL symbols?

Question 9.

a) How many rows had all IDENTICAL symbols?

b) Which row(s) had NON-IDENTICAL symbols?

Question 10.

a) How many rows had all IDENTICAL symbols?

b) Which row(s) had NON-IDENTICAL symbols?

Question 11.

Question 12.

Question 13.

Question 14

Question 15.

Question 11.

a) How many rows had all IDENTICAL symbols?

b) Which row(s) had NON-IDENTICAL symbols?

Question 12.

a) How many rows had NON-IDENTICAL symbols?

b) Which row(s) had all IDENTICAL symbols?

Question 13.

a) How many rows had all IDENTICAL symbols?

b) Which row(s) had NON-IDENTICAL symbols?

Question 14.

a) How many rows had all IDENTICAL symbols?

b) Which row(s) had NON-IDENTICAL symbols?

Question 15.

a) How many rows had all IDENTICAL symbols?

b) Which row(s) had NON-IDENTICAL symbols?

ANSWERS OVERLEAF

Q1.

a) 2

b) 1 and 3

Q2.

a) 2

b) 2 and 4

Q3.

a) 3

b) 1

Q4.

a) 4

b) 0

Q5.

a) 2

b) 2 and 3

Q6.

a) 1

b) 1, 2, and 4

Q7.

a) 3

b) 1

Q8.

a) 0

b) 1, 2, 3, and 4

Q9.

a) 3

b) 4

Q10.

a) 1

b) 1, 2, and 3

Q11.

a) 1

b) 2, 3, and 4

Q12.

a) 3

b) 2

Q13.

a) 2

b) 3 and 4

Q14.

a) 2

b) 1 and 2

Q15.

a) 2

b) 1 and 2

Error Analysis – Test 2

Look at all 4 rows below. Make a mental note of which rows contain identical symbols and which contain non-identical symbols. Answer one question (part a and part b) at a time. You have 30 seconds before you need to turn over to the next page and answer the questions.

Question 1.

1														
2														
3														
4														

Question 2.

1														
2														
3														
4														

Question 3.

1														
2														
3														
4														

Question 4.

1														
2														
3														
4														

Question 5.

1														
2														
3														
4														

Question 1.

a) How many rows had NON-IDENTICAL symbols?

b) Which row(s) had all IDENTICAL symbols?

Question 2.

a) How many rows had all IDENTICAL symbols?

b) Which row(s) had NON-IDENTICAL symbols?

Question 3.

a) How many rows had all IDENTICAL symbols?

b) Which row(s) had NON-IDENTICAL symbols?

Question 4.

a) How many rows had all IDENTICAL symbols?

b) Which row(s) had NON-IDENTICAL symbols?

Question 5.

a) How many rows had NON-IDENTICAL symbols?

b) Which row(s) had all IDENTICAL symbols?

Question 6.

#														
1	🖹	🖹	♍	●	🖹	🖹	♎		🖹	🖹	♍	●	🖹	🖹	♎
2	⌘	◆	♓	☐	●	●		⌘	◆	♓	☐	●	●
3	◆	◆	♓	●	☐	❖	❖		❖	◆	♓	●	☐	❖	❖
4	◆	🖹	⌛	🖱	🗐	🖹	☐		◆	🖹	⌛	🖱	🗐	🖹	☐

Question 7.

#														
1	☐	♎	♐	☐	◆	○	■		☐	♎	♐	☐	◆	○	■
2	♎	♎	☼	☞	◆	◆	■		♎	♎	☼	☞	◆	◆	■
3	◆	◆	❖	🖹	♐	♐	●		◆	◆	❖	🖹	♐	♐	♌
4	🖹	⌛	🖹	🖱	❄	✌	☺		🖹	⌛	🖹	🖱	❄	✌	☺

Question 8.

#														
1	🖺	🖹	◆	◆	●	●	○		🖺	🖹	◆	◆	●	●	○
2	🖱	🖺	🖹	🖱	❖	❖	☹		🖱	🖺	🖹	🖱	❖	❖	☹
3	◆	■	☐	♀	♌	♎	▭		◆	■	☐	♀	♌	♎	▭
4	🖱	🖹	🖹	♠	♍	●	☐		🖱	🖹	🖹	♠	♍	●	☐

Question 9.

#														
1	▣	▣	▭	♀	☚	⌛	●		▣	▣	▭	●	♐	⌛	●
2	♏	♌	♐	☐	♏	◆	◆		♎	♌	♐	☐	●	◆	◆
3	ℯℴ	◆	⚰	🖹	🗐	◆	🖹		ℯℴ	◆	⚰	🖹	🗐	◆	🖹
4	🗐	◆	♎	🖹	⌨	🖺	●		🗐	◆	♎	🖹	⌨	🖺	●

Question 10.

#														
1	🖺	◆	♎	🖺	ℯℴ	⌛	⌛		🖺	◆	♎	🖺	ℯℴ	⌛	⌛
2	🖺	🖹	🖹	🖹	☺	☹	⚰		🖺	🖹	🖹	🖹	☺	☹	❖
3	◆	◆	♠	●	🖐	☹	❖		◆	◆	♠	●	🖐	☹	❖
4	🖹	☺	☹	☼	🖐	✍	☐		🖹	☺	☹	☼	🖐	✍	☐

Question 6.

a) How many rows had all IDENTICAL symbols?

b) Which row(s) had NON-IDENTICAL symbols?

Question 7

a) How many rows had all IDENTICAL symbols?

b) Which row(s) had NON-IDENTICAL symbols?

Question 8.

a) How many rows had all IDENTICAL symbols?

b) Which row(s) had NON-IDENTICAL symbols?

Question 9.

a) How many rows had NON-IDENTICAL symbols?

b) Which row(s) had all IDENTICAL symbols?

Question 10.

a) How many rows had all IDENTICAL symbols?

b) Which row(s) had NON-IDENTICAL symbols?

Question 11.

Question 12.

Question 13.

Question 14.

Question 15.

Question 11.

a) How many rows had all IDENTICAL symbols?

b) Which row(s) had NON-IDENTICAL symbols?

Question 12.

a) How many rows had all IDENTICAL symbols?

b) Which row(s) had NON-IDENTICAL symbols?

Question 13.

a) How many rows had NON-IDENTICAL symbols?

b) Which row(s) had all IDENTICAL symbols?

Question 14.

a) How many rows had all IDENTICAL symbols?

b) Which row(s) had NON-IDENTICAL symbols?

Question 15.

a) How many rows had all IDENTICAL symbols?

b) Which row(s) had NON-IDENTICAL symbols?

ANSWERS OVERLEAF

Q1.
a) 0
b) 1, 2, 3 and 4

Q2.
a) 3
b) 3

Q3.
a) 2
b) 1 and 4

Q4.
a) 3
b) 4

Q5.
a) 1
b) 1, 2, and 3

Q6.
a) 3
b) 3

Q7.
a) 3
b) 3

Q8.
a) 4
b) 0

Q9.
a) 2
b) 3 and 4

Q10.
a) 3
b) 2

Q11.
a) 4
b) 0

Q12.
a) 3
b) 4

Q13.
a) 1
b) 1, 2, and 3

Q14.
a) 4
b) 0

Q15.
a) 3
b) 1

Error Analysis – Test 3

Look at all 4 rows below. Make a mental note of which rows contain identical symbols and which contain non-identical symbols. Answer one question (part a and part b) at a time. You have 30 seconds before you need to turn over to the next page and answer the questions.

Question 1.

#															
1	♍	♎	♎	♎	♑	♒	⅋		♍	♎	♎	♎	♑	♒	⅋
2	●	■	◆	♎	♏	◆	♋		●	■	♐	●	♏	◆	♋
3	◆	⊠	⅋	◮	♏	◆	♋		◆	⊠	⅋	◮	♏	◆	♋
4	□	⊠	□	♋	□	⌨	●		□	⊠	□	♋	□	⌨	●

Question 2.

#															
1	♎	■	♍	♎	♊	⅋	□		♎	■	♍	♎	♊	⅋	□
2	♏	□	◆	♋	◮	▯	⊠		♏	□	◆	♋	◮	▯	⊠
3	▤	◆	●	♋	◆	♍	♎		▤	◆	●	♋	◆	♍	♎
4	▤	▯	⌂	♊	⅋	♌	⊠		▤	♒	⌂	♊	⅋	♌	⊠

Question 3.

#															
1	♎	▯	▤	●	□	◆	◆		♎	▯	▤	●	□	◆	◆
2	▤	♨	♑	♒	♊	⅋	□		▤	♨	♑	♒	♊	⅋	□
3	□	⌘	⅋	□	◆	♒	♊		□	⌘	⅋	□	◆	♒	♊
4	♎	■	○	♋	◆	♏	●		♎	■	○	■	◆	♏	●

Question 4.

#															
1	⌨	⌂	▤	♐	♒	♍	⌘		⌨	⌂	▤	♐	♒	♍	⌘
2	◆	♑	⅋	□	⊠	◆	♏		◆	♓	⅋	□	⊠	◆	♏
3	◆	❖	◆	♓	◆	◆	♋		◆	❖	◆	♓	◆	◆	♋
4	♏	♨	⌂	▤	▤	⌨	◆		♏	♨	⌂	▤	▤	⌨	◆

Question 5.

#															
1	◆	♓	□	♨	❖	♋	♨		◆	♓	□	♨	❖	♋	♨
2	⅋	❖	♏	◆	♋	○	◆		⅋	❖	♏	◆	♋	○	◆
3	♓	❖	♒	■	⅋	●	□		♓	❖	♒	■	⅋	●	□
4	⌂	□	◆	♍	♊	♅	▤		⌂	□	◆	♍	♊	♅	▤

Question 1.

a) How many rows had all IDENTICAL symbols?

b) Which row(s) had NON-IDENTICAL symbols?

Question 2.

a) Which row(s) had all IDENTICAL symbols?

b) How many rows had NON-IDENTICAL symbols?

Question 3.

a) Which row(s) had all IDENTICAL symbols?

b) How many rows had NON-IDENTICAL symbols?

Question 4.

a) How many rows had all IDENTICAL symbols?

b) Which row(s) had NON-IDENTICAL symbols?

Question 5.

a) How many rows had all IDENTICAL symbols?

b) Which row(s) had NON-IDENTICAL symbols?

Question 6.

Question 7.

Question 8.

Question 9.

Question 10.

Question 6.

a) How many rows had all IDENTICAL symbols?

b) Which row(s) had NON-IDENTICAL symbols?

Question 7

a) Which row(s) had all IDENTICAL symbols?

b) How many rows had NON-IDENTICAL symbols?

Question 8.

a) Which row(s) had all IDENTICAL symbols?

b) How many rows had NON-IDENTICAL symbols?

Question 9.

a) How many rows had all IDENTICAL symbols?

b) Which row(s) had NON-IDENTICAL symbols?

Question 10.

a) How many rows had all IDENTICAL symbols?

b) Which row(s) had NON-IDENTICAL symbols?

Question 11.

1	♋	♍	♒	er	&	●	□		♋	♍	♒	er	&	●	□
2	♏	⊡	♒	♎	◆	♋	□		♏	⊡	♒	♎	◆	♋	□
3	🗐	♒	er	&	●	□	♎		🗐	♒	er	&	●	□	♎
4	☺	☝	☼	💣	☠	☹	✋		☺	☝	☼	💣	☠	☹	✋

Question 12.

1	☞	💣	☠	◆	☹	☺	♋		☞	💣	☠	💣	☹	☺	♋
2	☝	♑	♒	er	◆	☒	♋		☝	♑	♒	er	◆	☒	♋
3	🗐	♑	er	♎	♏	◆	♎		🗐	●	er	♎	♏	◆	♎
4	🗐	❖	♒	er	♋	⊡	◻		🗐	❖	♒	er	♋	□	◻

Question 13.

1	▯	🖱	♐	♎	◆	♌	&		▯	🖱	♐	♎	◆	♌	&
2	□	☒	☹	☺	☝	☝	☚		□	☒	☹	☺	☝	☝	☚
3	❄	☹	☺	✌	👇	☠	☺		❄	☹	☺	✌	👇	☠	☺
4	✈	☹	☝	💣	☠	☝	☝		✈	☹	☝	💣	☠	☝	☝

Question 14.

1	♪	☼	♒	er	&	●	●		♪	☼	♒	er	&	●	●
2	◆	◆	♋	◆	⊡	◆	❖		❖	◆	♋	◆	⊡	◆	❖
3	⏳	🗐	🖹	er	&	●	❖		⏳	🗐	🖹	er	&	●	❖
4	♒	◆	♐	♒	er	&	●		♒	❖	♐	♒	er	&	●

Question 15.

1	▯	🖱	♎	♏	♐	◆	♒		▯	🖱	♎	♏	♐	◆	♒
2	♓	□	◆	❖	♎	♏	◆		&	□	◆	❖	♌	♏	◆
3	◆	⊡	er	◆	♋	♍	♑		◆	⊡	er	◆	♋	♍	♑
4	□	◻	⌘	⌘	❖	●	✌		□	◻	⌘	❖	❖	●	✌

Question 11.

a) How many rows had all IDENTICAL symbols?

b) Which row(s) had NON-IDENTICAL symbols?

Question 12.

a) Which row(s) had all IDENTICAL symbols?

b) How many rows had NON-IDENTICAL symbols?

Question 13.

a) Which row(s) had all IDENTICAL symbols?

b) How many rows had NON-IDENTICAL symbols?

Question 14.

a) How many rows had all IDENTICAL symbols?

b) Which row(s) had NON-IDENTICAL symbols?

Question 15.

a) How many rows had all IDENTICAL symbols?

b) Which row(s) had NON-IDENTICAL symbols?

ANSWERS OVERLEAF

Q1.
a) 3
b) 2

Q2.
a) 1, 2, and 3
b) 1

Q3.
a) 1, 2, and 3
b) 1

Q4.
a) 3
b) 2

Q5.
a) 4
b) 0

Q6.
a) 3
b) 2

Q7.
a) 4
b) 3

Q8.
a) 1, 4
b) 2

Q9.
a) 2
b) 2, 4

Q10.
a) 3
b) 4

Q11.
a) 4
b) 0

Q12.
a) 2
b) 3

Q13.
a) 1, 2, 3, and 4
b) 0

Q14.
a) 2
b) 2, 4

Q15.
a) 2
b) 2, 4

Error Analysis – Test 4

Look at all 4 rows below. Make a mental note of which rows contain identical symbols and which contain non-identical symbols. Answer one question (part a and part b) at a time. You have 30 seconds before you need to turn over to the next page and answer the questions.

Question 1.

#	Left row							#	Right row						
1	◫	☌	◆	☺	☠	▢	♏	1	◫	☌	◆	☺	☠	▢	♏
2	♈	&	●	○	♎	◆	♏	2	♈	&	●	○	♎	◆	♏
3	♑	♒	♈	&	▢	♎	♋	3	☠	♒	✋	&	▢	♎	♋
4	♄	♅	☹	▢	◆	♎	♏	4	♄	♅	☹	▢	◆	♎	♏

Question 2.

#	Left row							#	Right row						
1	▢	◆	◹	♈	&	●	○	1	▢	◆	◹	♈	&	●	○
2	◆	▢	▢	◆	♈	&	☺	2	◆	▢	▢	◆	♈	&	☺
3	☒	◹	◆	♏	♒	&	●	3	☒	◹	◆	♏	♒	&	●
4	◫	♒	♈	&	●	☒	♋	4	◫	♒	♈	&	●	☒	♋

Question 3.

#	Left row							#	Right row						
1	◫	♈	&	◆	☒	◆	◆	1	◫	♈	&	◆	☒	◆	◆
2	▢	◆	♒	&	▢	♏	☒	2	▢	◆	⌘	&	▢	♏	☒
3	❖	&	●	♓	▢	▢	◆	3	●	&	●	♓	▢	▢	◆
4	♋	▢	▢	♏	▢	☒	♒	4	♋	▢	▢	♏	▢	☒	☹

Question 4.

#	Left row							#	Right row						
1	◹	♈	&	◆	♏	☒	♓	1	◹	♈	&	◆	♏	☒	♓
2	▢	☒	♓	▢	▢	♍	♋	2	▢	☒	♓	▢	▢	♍	♋
3	▢	☒	♒	♈	☹	☙	✌	3	▢	☒	♒	♈	☹	☙	❄
4	⌘	▨	▤	♈	&	■	↗	4	⌘	↗	▤	♈	&	■	↗

Question 5.

#	Left row							#	Right row						
1	◫	♒	☏	▤	◆	♋	♌	1	◫	♒	☏	▤	◆	♋	♌
2	♏	♑	♒	◆	♓	▢	▢	2	♏	♑	♒	◆	♓	▢	▢
3	⌘	❖	▢	◆	♋	◆	◹	3	❖	❖	▢	◆	♋	◆	◹
4	▢	♓	▢	♒	&	☒	♏	4	▢	♓	◆	♒	&	☒	♏

Question 1.

a) How many rows had all IDENTICAL symbols?

b) Which row(s) had NON-IDENTICAL symbols?

Question 2.

a) Which row(s) had all IDENTICAL symbols?

b) How many rows had NON-IDENTICAL symbols?

Question 3.

a) Which row(s) had all IDENTICAL symbols?

b) How many rows had NON-IDENTICAL symbols?

Question 4.

a) How many rows had all IDENTICAL symbols?

b) Which row(s) had NON-IDENTICAL symbols?

Question 5.

a) How many rows had all IDENTICAL symbols?

b) Which row(s) had NON-IDENTICAL symbols?

Question 6.

Question 7.

Question 8.

Question 9.

Question 10.

Question 6.

a) How many rows had all IDENTICAL symbols?

b) Which row(s) had NON-IDENTICAL symbols?

Question 7.

a) Which row(s) had all IDENTICAL symbols?

b) How many rows had NON-IDENTICAL symbols?

Question 8.

a) Which row(s) had all IDENTICAL symbols?

b) How many rows had NON-IDENTICAL symbols?

Question 9.

a) How many rows had all IDENTICAL symbols?

b) Which row(s) had NON-IDENTICAL symbols?

Question 10.

a) How many rows had all IDENTICAL symbols?

b) Which row(s) had NON-IDENTICAL symbols?

Question 11.

1															
2															
3															
4															

Question 12.

1															
2															
3															
4															

Question 13.

1															
2															
3															
4															

Question 14.

1															
2															
3															
4															

Question 15.

1															
2															
3															
4															

Question 11.

a) How many rows had all IDENTICAL symbols?

b) Which row(s) had NON-IDENTICAL symbols?

Question 12.

a)   Which row(s) had all IDENTICAL symbols?

b) How many rows had NON-IDENTICAL symbols?

Question 13.

a)   Which row(s) had all IDENTICAL symbols?

b) How many rows had NON-IDENTICAL symbols?

Question 14.

a)   How many rows had all IDENTICAL symbols?

b) Which row(s) had NON-IDENTICAL symbols?

Question 15.

a) How many rows had all IDENTICAL symbols?

b) Which row(s) had NON-IDENTICAL symbols?

ANSWERS OVERLEAF

Q1.
a) 3
b) 3

Q2.
a) 1, 2, 3, and 4
b) 0

Q3.
a) 1
b) 3

Q4.
a) 2
b) 3, 4

Q5.
a) 2
b) 3, 4

Q6.
a) 2
b) 2, 3

Q7.
a) 1, 3
b) 2

Q8.
a) 1, 3
b) 2

Q9.
a) 3
b) 2

Q10.
a) 1
b) 1, 2, and 3

Q11.
a) 2
b) 1, 4

Q12.
a) 2
b) 3

Q13.
a) 1
b) 3

Q14.
a) 1
b) 1, 3, and 4

Q15.
a) 3
b) 3

Number
Reasoning

The Number Reasoning Test assesses your ability to calculate and memorise a series of simple sums, and then answer questions based on them. While this might sound easy, you'll have to answer a lot of questions very quickly, and also remember numbers in your head before answering the questions.

For each question, you will be given four sums. You are not allowed to write your answers down, so you will need to calculate them in your head, and then memorise the answers. YYou will have 30 seconds to do this. You will then turn the page over, and answer two questions based on the answers to the sums.

Let's take a look at an example:

Sample Question 1.			
A	12 × 2	**B**	15 ÷ 3
C	4 × 3	**D**	8 × 2

Start by quickly answering all four of the sums:

A) $12 \times 2 = 24$

B) $15 \div 3 = 5$

C) $4 \times 3 = 12$

D) $8 \times 2 = 16$

Once all four sums have been answered, you will need to turn the page and answer the questions. Here's an example:

Sample Question 1.	
a) Which answer contained a single digit?	
b) Which answer was 16?	

You need to pick the sum which matches the answer. Let's start with a):

a) Which answer contained a single digit?

Of all the answer options, only one answer contains a single digit:

   B) $15 \div 3 = 5$

Therefore, the answer to this question is B.

Sample Question 1.	
a) Which answer contained a single digit?	B
b) Which answer was 16?	

Next, we move onto b):

b) Which answer was 16?

Only one answer equals 16:

D) 8 × 2 = 16

Therefore, the correct answer is D.

Sample Question 1.	
a) Which answer contained a single digit?	B
b) Which answer was 16?	D

Therefore, we have our answers, and can move onto the next question.

As a final tip, make sure that you answer all four of the sums and memorise them before looking at the questions. If you don't, you run the risk of lacking one of the answers that you need!

Give the following sample tests a try. Make sure that you memorise the answers before moving onto the questions.

TEST 1 WILL BEGIN ON THE NEXT PAGE

Number Reasoning – Test 1

Answer each question one at a time. Work out the calculations in the table. Do not write your answers down. You have 30 seconds to work out and memorise the answers before turning the page for the question.

Question 1.			
A	19 × 3	**B**	66 ÷ 2
C	4 × 14	**D**	15 × 2

Question 2.			
A	12 × 11	**B**	12 × 5
C	48 ÷ 4	**D**	25 ÷ 5

Question 3.			
A	67 – 9	**B**	40 ÷ 4
C	27 ÷ 3	**D**	36 + 6

Question 4.			
A	12 × 4	**B**	500 ÷ 2
C	20 × 5	**D**	16 – 12

Question 5.			
A	7 – 1	**B**	13 × 2
C	12 + 35	**D**	64 ÷ 8

Question 1.

a) Which answer contained identical digits?

b) Which answer was 30?

Question 2.

a) Which answer contained just 1 digit?

b) Which answer was 60?

Question 3.

a) Which was the only odd answer?

b) Which answer equalled 10?

Question 4.

a) Which answer equalled exactly 100?

b) Which was the only 2 digit answer?

Question 5.

a) Which answer contained the digit 7?

b) Which answer had 2 even digits?

Question 6.			
A	56 ÷ 7	B	39 – 3
C	22 × 3	D	18 × 2

Question 7.			
A	74 – 20	B	20 × 30
C	6 + 26	D	55 – 10

Question 8.			
A	11 × 3	B	36 – 18
C	25 × 6	D	20 ÷ 4

Question 9.			
A	67 – 17	B	99 – 87
C	24 + 30	D	60 ÷ 10

Question 10.			
A	96 – 21	B	200 ÷ 10
C	11 × 5	D	75 – 14

Question 6.

a) Which answer was identical to answer B?

b) Which answer contained just 1 digit?

Question 7.

a) Which answer was the highest?

b) Which was the only odd answer?

Question 8.

a) Which answer contained TWO identical digits?

b) Which answer was greater than 100?

Question 9.

a) Which answer was exactly 50?

b) Which answer only contained 1 digit?

Question 10.

a) Which was the only even number?

b) Which answer was the lowest?

Question 11.			
A	21 × 2	**B**	99 ÷ 11
C	54 ÷ 6	**D**	100 − 16

Question 12.			
A	86 − 14	**B**	60 ÷ 3
C	18 ÷ 9	**D**	152 − 49

Question 13.			
A	28 ÷ 2	**B**	49 − 19
C	100 ÷ 5	**D**	25 − 14

Question 14.			
A	36 ÷ 6	**B**	43 − 9
C	12 × 3	**D**	23 × 2

Question 15.			
A	99 − 33	**B**	80 − 27
C	14 + 30	**D**	100 ÷ 2

Question 11.

a) Which answer was identical to answer C?

b) Which answer was the highest?

Question 12.

a) Which answer had the lowest numerical value?

b) Which answer contained 3 digits?

Question 13.

a) Which answer contained the digit 4?

b) Which answer equalled the highest numerical value?

Question 14.

a) Which answer contained just 1 digit?

b) Which answer equalled 36?

Question 15.

a) Which answer contained TWO ODD digits?

b) Which answer equalled LESS than 50?

ANSWERS OVERLEAF

Q1.
a) B
b) D

Q2.
a) D
b) B

Q3.
a) C
b) B

Q4.
a) C
b) A

Q5.
a) C
b) B

Q6.
a) D
b) A

Q7.
a) B
b) D

Q8.
a) A
b) C

Q9.
a) A
b) D

Q10.
a) B
b) B

Q11.
a) B
b) D

Q12.
a) C
b) D

Q13.
a) A
b) B

Q14.
a) A
b) C

Q15.
a) B
b) C

Number Reasoning – Test 2

Answer each question one at a time. Work out the calculations in the table. Do not write your answers down. You have 30 seconds to work out and memorise the answers before turning the page for the question.

Question 1.			
A	10 × 5	**B**	100 ÷ 2
C	66 ÷ 2	**D**	10 – 1

Question 2.			
A	30 ÷ 2	**B**	4 × 5
C	28 ÷ 4	**D**	18 × 11

Question 3.			
A	22 – 7	**B**	78 ÷ 2
C	8 × 3	**D**	14 ÷ 2

Question 4.			
A	12 × 3	**B**	90 ÷ 2
C	7 × 4	**D**	88 – 27

Question 5.			
A	44 ÷ 2	**B**	60 ÷ 3
C	8 × 2	**D**	30 ÷ 3

Question 1.

a) Which answer contained just 1 digit?

b) Which answer contained two identical digits?

Question 2.

a) Which answer contained just 1 digit?

b) Which answer equalled 20?

Question 3.

a) Which answer equalled LESS than 10?

b) Which answer equalled the HIGHEST in numerical value?

Question 4.

a) Which answer equalled 28?

b) Which answer contained the digit 5?

Question 5.

a) Which answer equalled the LOWEST in numerical value?

b) Which answer equalled 10?

Question 6.			
A	16 – 9	**B**	60 – 9
C	33 × 2	**D**	19 × 3

Question 7.			
A	22 – 9	**B**	22 ÷ 2
C	15 – 8	**D**	4 × 4

Question 8.			
A	9 × 4	**B**	76 ÷ 2
C	13 + 9	**D**	8 × 5

Question 9.			
A	88 – 9	**B**	62 + 22
C	21 + 9	**D**	19 × 5

Question 10.			
A	21 × 4	**B**	10 × 5
C	33 + 8	**D**	32 × 2

Question 6.

a) Which answer contained just 1 digit?

b) Which answer equalled to MORE than 60?

Question 7.

a) Which answer contained just 1 digit?

b) Which answer equalled 16?

Question 8.

a) Which answer equalled MORE than 38?

b) Which answer equalled the HIGHEST in numerical value?

Question 9.

a) Which answer equalled 95?

b) Which answer equalled the LOWEST in numerical value?

Question 10.

a) Which answer equalled 41?

b) Which answer did NOT contain the digit 4?

Question 11.			
A	7 × 3	**B**	32 ÷ 2
C	88 ÷ 4	**D**	11 + 8

Question 12.			
A	33 + 21	**B**	22 ÷ 11
C	30 ÷ 3	**D**	24 + 6

Question 13.			
A	8 × 3	**B**	12 × 3
C	99 ÷ 11	**D**	88 + 6

Question 14.			
A	21 × 3	**B**	32 × 2
C	48 ÷ 2	**D**	4 × 7

Question 15.			
A	55 − 7	**B**	16 ÷ 4
C	13 × 3	**D**	32 ÷ 2

Question 11.

a) Which answer equalled 16?

b) Which answer equalled the HIGHEST in numerical value?

Question 12.

a) Which answer equalled 54?

b) Which answer equalled LESS than 10?

Question 13.

a) Which answer equalled 9?

b) Which answer equalled the HIGHEST in numerical value?

Question 14.

a) Which answer contained the digit 3?

b) Which answer equalled MORE than 63?

Question 15.

a) Which answer equalled 4?

b) Which answer equalled 16?

ANSWERS OVERLEAF

Q1.
a) D
b) C

Q2.
a) C
b) B

Q3.
a) D
b) B

Q4.
a) C
b) B

Q5.
a) D
b) D

Q6.
a) A
b) C

Q7.
a) C
b) D

Q8.
a) D
b) D

Q9.
a) D
b) C

Q10.
a) C
b) B

Q11.
a) B
b) C

Q12.
a) A
b) B

Q13.
a) C
b) D

Q14.
a) A
b) B

Q15.
a) B
b) D

Number Reasoning – Test 3

Answer each question one at a time. Work out the calculations in the table. Do not write your answers down. You have 30 seconds to work out and memorise the answers before turning the page for the question.

Question 1.			
A	3×7	B	$18 + 4$
C	18×2	D	$24 \div 2$

Question 2.			
A	10×3	B	5×3
C	$80 \div 4$	D	$23 + 7$

Question 3.			
A	$22 - 9$	B	$33 + 22$
C	$41 + 9$	D	25×5

Question 4.			
A	41×3	B	4×5
C	$14 + 8$	D	16×3

Question 5.			
A	13×3	B	12×2
C	$40 \div 4$	D	4×11

Question 1.

a) Which answer equalled an odd number?

b) Which answer did NOT contain the digit 2?

Question 2.

a) Which answer did NOT contain the digit 0?

b) Which answer equalled the LOWEST in numerical value?

Question 3.

a) Which answer equalled 55?

b) Which answer equalled the LOWEST in numerical value?

Question 4.

a) Which answer contained 3 digits?

b) Which answer equalled the HIGHEST in numerical value?

Question 5.

a) Which answer contained two identical digits?

b) Which answer equalled LESS than 20?

Question 6.			
A	9 × 4	B	9 × 5
C	30 + 8	D	20 × 3

Question 7.			
A	7 × 3	B	18 + 6
C	23 × 2	D	42 ÷ 2

Question 8.			
A	19 − 9	B	30 ÷ 2
C	14 − 9	D	3 × 4

Question 9.			
A	70 − 30	B	22 + 28
C	24 + 6	D	33 × 2

Question 10.			
A	50 − 30	B	15 + 17
C	45 + 6	D	12 × 3

Question 6.

a) Which answer equalled 36?

b) Which answer contained the digit 0?

Question 7.

a) Which answer equalled the same as A?

b) Which answer did NOT contain the digit 2?

Question 8.

a) Which answer contained just 1 digit?

b) Which answer equalled 15?

Question 9.

a) Which answer equalled 30?

b) Which answer equalled the HIGHEST in numerical value?

Question 10.

a) Which answer contained the digit 0?

b) Which answer equalled the LOWEST in numerical value?

Question 11.			
A	6 × 3	**B**	18 ÷ 6
C	4 × 4	**D**	22 − 10

Question 12.			
A	12 × 3	**B**	14 × 2
C	20 ÷ 4	**D**	4 × 12

Question 13.			
A	33 × 3	**B**	32 ÷ 2
C	38 − 7	**D**	18 + 3

Question 14.			
A	18 − 7	**B**	21 ÷ 3
C	4 × 3	**D**	22 ÷ 2

Question 15.			
A	20 − 19	**B**	100 − 9
C	45 × 2	**D**	15 × 3

Question 11.

a) Which answer equalled 18?

b) Which answer equalled an ODD number?

Question 12.

a) Which answer equalled 5?

b) Which answer equalled MORE than 40?

Question 13.

a) Which answer equalled the LOWEST in numerical value?

b) Which answer did NOT contain the digit 1?

Question 14.

a) Which answer equalled LESS than 10?

b) Which answer equalled the HIGHEST in numerical value?

Question 15.

a) Which answer contained just 1 digit?

b) Which answer equalled to MORE than 90?

ANSWERS OVERLEAF

Q1.
a) A
b) C

Q2.
a) B
b) B

Q3.
a) B
b) A

Q4.
a) A
b) A

Q5.
a) D
b) C

Q6.
a) A
b) D

Q7.
a) D
b) C

Q8.
a) C
b) B

Q9.
a) C
b) D

Q10.
a) A
b) A

Q11.
a) A
b) B

Q12.
a) C
b) D

Q13.
a) B
b) A

Q14.
a) B
b) C

Q15.
a) A
b) B

Number Reasoning – Test 4

Answer each question one at a time. Work out the calculations in the table. Do not write your answers down. You have 30 seconds to work out and memorise the answers before turning the page for the question.

Question 1.			
A	6 × 7	**B**	70 ÷ 2
C	98 ÷ 2	**D**	38 + 8

Question 2.			
A	21 – 7	**B**	15 ÷ 3
C	12 × 3	**D**	24 ÷ 2

Question 3.			
A	41 + 21	**B**	55 ÷ 11
C	30 ÷ 3	**D**	14 + 6

Question 4.			
A	6 × 11	**B**	16 × 3
C	99 ÷ 9	**D**	4 × 8

Question 5.			
A	21 ÷ 7	**B**	19 + 3
C	16 × 2	**D**	20 ÷ 10

Question 1.

a) Which answer equalled 35?

b) Which answer equalled the HIGHEST in numerical value?

Question 2.

a) Which answer equalled 36?

b) Which answer equalled 12?

Question 3.

a) Which answer equalled 62?

b) Which answer equalled LESS than 10?

Question 4.

a) Which answer contained the digit 1?

b) Which answer equalled MORE than 50?

Question 5.

a) Which answer equalled an odd number?

b) Which answer did NOT contain the digit 2?

Question 6.			
A	12 × 3	**B**	22 + 2
C	32 ÷ 4	**D**	9 × 3

Question 7.			
A	23 × 3	**B**	9 × 11
C	80 ÷ 5	**D**	87 + 7

Question 8.			
A	40 × 10	**B**	45 × 3
C	60 ÷ 6	**D**	103 + 7

Question 9.			
A	33 × 3	**B**	7 × 5
C	44 + 8	**D**	22 × 6

Question 10.			
A	14 − 9	**B**	20 + 24
C	4 + 3	**D**	35 × 3

Question 6.

a) Which answer contained one digit?

b) Which answer equalled MORE than 30?

Question 7.

a) Which answer equalled 16?

b) Which answer equalled the HIGHEST in numerical value?

Question 8.

a) Which answer did NOT contain the digit 0?

b) Which answer equalled the HIGHEST in numerical value?

Question 9.

a) Which answer contained 3 digits?

b) Which answer equalled the LOWEST in numerical value?

Question 10.

a) Which answer equalled 44?

b) Which answer equalled the LOWEST in numerical value?

Question 11.			
A	11 × 4	**B**	66 − 23
C	42 + 8	**D**	14 × 3

Question 12.			
A	12 × 4	**B**	24 × 2
C	15 + 7	**D**	19 × 3

Question 13.			
A	13 × 2	**B**	16 + 6
C	46 ÷ 2	**D**	60 ÷ 2

Question 14.			
A	72 ÷ 2	**B**	34 × 3
C	48 + 12	**D**	12 × 3

Question 15.			
A	35 × 3	**B**	12 + 87
C	12 × 2	**D**	30 ÷ 3

Question 11.

a) Which answer equalled 42?

b) Which answer did NOT contain the digit 4?

Question 12.

a) Which answer equalled 57?

b) Which answer was identical to answer A?

Question 13.

a) Which answer equalled an ODD number?

b) Which answer did NOT contain the digit 2?

Question 14.

a) Which answer equalled 60?

b) Which answer was identical to answer D?

Question 15.

a) Which answer equalled 24?

b) Which answer did NOT contain 2 digits?

ANSWERS OVERLEAF

Q1.
a) B
b) C

Q2.
a) C
b) D

Q3.
a) A
b) B

Q4.
a) C
b) A

Q5.
a) A
b) A

Q6.
a) C
b) A

Q7.
a) C
b) B

Q8.
a) B
b) A

Q9.
a) D
b) B

Q10.
a) B
b) A

Q11.
a) D
b) C

Q12.
a) D
b) B

Q13.
a) C
b) D

Q14.
a) C
b) A

Q15.
a) C
b) A

A Few Final Words

Congratulations! You've made it to the end of this workbook. You should now be more confident than ever with regards to the Army Aptitude Tests. Additionally, you're in a great position to continue practising for the range of questions that you might face in the Army Aptitude Tests.

Here are some final tips before you go:

For Error Analysis, make sure that you carefully read every single symbol for each row. Sometimes, symbols will look similar, and this will catch a lot of careless candidates out. Don't be one of those applicants. Make sure that you strike the perfect balance between accuracy and speed.

When it comes to Number Reasoning, try not to get complacent. While the sums are often quite easy to figure out in your head, the questions themselves can be extremely tricky. Rather than just remembering the answers to the sums as full numbers (e.g. 66 or "sixty-six"), think of them also as a pair of single digits (e.g. "six and six"). Doing this will give you the best chance of accurately remembering all of the digits. This is vital, since you could be asked a question about single digits, rather than the numbers as a whole.

The majority of candidates who pass the British Army selection process have a number of common factors. These are as follows:

1. They believe in themselves.

The first factor is self-belief. Regardless of what anyone tells you, you can pass the selection process and you can achieve high scores. Just like any job of this nature, you have to be prepared to work hard in order to be successful. You will notice that the Army Aptitude Tests are tough. Make sure you have the self-belief to pass the selection process and fill your mind with positive thoughts.

2. They prepare fully.

The second factor is preparation. Those people who achieve in life prepare fully for every eventuality and that is what you must do when you apply to join the Army and sit the Army Aptitude Tests. Work very hard and especially concentrate on your weak areas. By comparing your answers to ours, identify the areas that you are weak on and go all out to improve them.

3. They persevere.

Perseverance is a fantastic word. Everybody comes across obstacles or setbacks in their life, but it is what you do about those setbacks that is important. If you fail at something, then ask yourself 'why' have I failed? This will allow you to improve for next time. If you keep improving and trying, success will eventually follow. Apply this same method of thinking when you apply to join the Army.

4. They are self-motivated.

How much do you want to join the Army? Do you want it, or do you really want it? When you apply to join the Army, you should want it more than anything in the world. Your levels of self-motivation will shine through when you walk into the AFCO and when you attend the interview. For the weeks and months leading up to the selection process, be motivated as best you can and always keep your fitness levels up as this will serve to increase your levels of motivation.

Work hard, stay focused, and secure your dream career.

The how2become team

The How2Become Team.

IMPROVE YOUR ARMED FORCES SCORES!

Our How2Become Armed Forces guides are the ULTIMATE revision resources to prepare you fully for joining the Army.

FOR MORE INFORMATION ON OUR ARMY GUIDES, PLEASE CHECK OUT THE FOLLOWING:

WWW.HOW2BECOME.COM

Printed in Great Britain
by Amazon